ENDURING WOMAN JOURNAL COLLECTION

Every Woman
In You Should
_____!

Emily Claudette Freeman

Every Woman In You Should _____! by Emily Claudette Freeman

All rights reserved. Printed in the United States of America.

No part of this book may be used or reproduced in any manner whatsoever, without written permission of the author or a legal representative; except in the case of quotations embodied in critical articles or reviews.

©November 2015, Emily Claudette Freeman
Graphic Design by Jenette Antonio Sityar

Published by Pecan Tree Publishing, Hollywood, Fl

www.pecantreebooks.com

Library of Congress: 2016931960

ISBN: 978-0-9888969-4-9

PECAN TREE PUBLISHING
Hollywood, Fl.
www.pecantreebooks.com

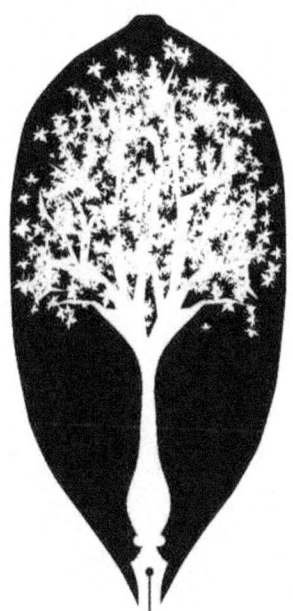

New Voices | New Styles | New Vision

Welcome Message

Every Woman In You Should _____ is the middle child in the Enduring Woman Journal Collection. She is special to me. You see I am a middle child. We are believed to be the most peculiar kids in the family dynamic. Isn't that a wonderful thing to be? Who wants to be average? The middle child is a big shaker of cayenne pepper on a table with no other condiments. We add spice!

That is what I am hoping you release as you write for your life in the second journal in this collection – spice. This journal is for the multi-dynamic woman who can live, dance, cry, rejoice and be at peace in all those things. She knows that just as she experiences life, life experiences her and thus she has a unique and thriving rhythm that leads her forth.

Every woman in you should be the woman she desires to be – even if that changes frequently. You are the definition of you and what God created you to be.

Step, slide, cha cha and mix it up – dance, girl – dance – every woman in you should!

Emily Claudette Freeman

Hey baby girl, what's that look about
Not down, not out .... No, no, no
Baby girl there's too much to dance about
That's right dance

Dance, baby girl
Every woman in you should dance, no matter the occasion

Dance,
when you're crying cause what's in your heart
Isn't adding up to what's in your face ...
That two step auntie Pearl taught you feels just fine

Dance,
when the tears leave tread marks in your Fashion Fair, Maybelline – Whatever ...
Let the breeze from your Chubby Checker twist blow them away

Dance, sister,
when you know he's gone for good – again – this time,
But you stay by the phone waiting for the call
Sweep his dust out the door, in the movement of your tango-a-solo

Dance, sweetheart,
when the muse that used to amuse you is gone
Cause somebody else is trying to take it.
There's a cha cha waiting to make you smile

Juke daughter, that's right – dance, baby girl,
When they tell you're not worth anything
Not a thing
You better know
It's a rare jewel that can tooty fruity life you

Dance, baby girl,
even your body is sore from the foolishness and strife
Of this thing called life
Even when your mind is pounding
Struggling in comprehension
Determining emotions that are more surreal
Than actual fantasy or reality

Every Woman in you Should _____ !

Even when you spirit seems to have laid down in the battle,
But your heart –
Still wants to go on

You gotta dance for the little girl tugging in your gut
That still wants to be held
Dance for the motherly warm hands that still want to hold on
To a baby growing and leaving quicker than a Charleston step

Dance for the lover
Who can't love you like you want to be loved
Because his beat wasn't designed for your rhythm

Dance, sister
When your wide hips, can't dip like they use to
And your sturdy hands don't give that hardy, happy pounding sound
Like Mahalia's used to
And your groove has grown weary and unresponsive to the natural drums
in your soul

Still dance, baby girl
Cut a rug or two for me and you

Cause no matter what,
I've got a song
And every song has a dance
And every dance loves to see a woman move
So…
Dance baby girl
Find a note that takes you away to the glory of you

Dance baby girl
Like this may be the last time, as old folks used to say

DANCE
Girl, dance
Every woman in you

Lover
Mother
Friend

Rejected
Joyous
Dejected

Uplifted
Upset
Perplexed

Remembered and
Forgotten

Every woman in you should dance
No matter what the occasion

Every Woman in you Should _____!

Every Woman in You Should Dance!

Psalm 149:3

Let them praise his name in the dance: let them sing praises unto him with the timbrel and harp.

So DANCE!

Every Woman in you Should _____!

Every Woman in you Should _____!

Every Woman in you Should _____!

Every Woman in you Should _____!

Every Woman In You Should Cry!

Psalms 30:5

For his anger endureth but a moment; in his favour is life: weeping may endure for a night, but joy cometh in the morning.

So CRY!

Every Woman in you Should _____!

Every Woman in you Should _____!

Every Woman in you Should _____!

Every Woman In You Should Live!

John 10:10

I am come that they might have life, and that they might have it more abundantly.

So LIVE!

Every Woman in you Should _____!

Every Woman in you Should _____!

Every Woman in you Should _____!

Every Woman In You Should Love!

Proverbs 31:25

Strength and honour are her clothing; and she shall rejoice in time to come.

So LOVE!

Every Woman in you Should _____!

Every Woman in you Should _____!

Every Woman in you Should _____!

Every Woman in you Should _____!

Every Woman In You Should Praise!

Phillippians 4:13

I can do all things through Christ which strengtheneth me.

So PRAISE!

Every Woman in you Should _____!

Every Woman in you Should _____!

Every Woman In You Should Prosper!

Psalms 24:1

The earth is the Lord's, and the fullness thereof; the world, and they that dwell therein.

So PROSPER!

Every Woman in you Should _____!

Every Woman in you Should _____!

Every Woman in you Should _____!

Every Woman In You Should Rejoice!

Romans 8:37

Nay, in all these things we are more than conquerors through him that loved us.

So REJOICE!

Every Woman in you Should _____!

Every Woman in you Should _____!

Every Woman in you Should _____!

Every Woman In You Should Release!

Psalms 55:22

Cast thy burden upon the Lord, and he shall sustain thee: he shall never suffer the righteous to be moved.

So RELEASE!

Every Woman in you Should _____!

Every Woman in you Should _____!

Every Woman in you Should _____!

Every Woman in you Should _____!

Every Woman In You Should Forgive!

Matthew 18:21

Then came Peter to him, and said, Lord, how oft shall my brother sin against me, and I forgive him? till seven times?

So FORGIVE!

Every Woman in you Should _____!

Every Woman in you Should _____!

Every Woman In You Should Smile!

Numbers 6:24-26

The Lord bless thee, and keep thee: The Lord make his face shine upon thee, and be gracious unto thee: The Lord lift up his countenance upon thee, and give thee peace.

So SMILE!

Every Woman in you Should _____!

Every Woman in you Should _____!

Every Woman In You Should Heal!

Isaiah 57:18

I have seen his ways, and will heal him: I will lead him also, and restore comforts unto him and to his mourners.

So Heal!

Every Woman in you Should _____!

Every Woman in you Should _____!

Every Woman in you Should _____ !

Every Woman in you Should _____!

Every Woman In You Should Give!

Genesis 1:15

And let them be for lights in the firmament of the heaven to give light upon the earth: and it was so.

So Give!

Every Woman in you Should _____!

Every Woman in you Should _____!

Every Woman in you Should _____!

Every Woman In You Should Desire!

Psalm 10:17

Lord, thou hast heard the desire of the humble: thou wilt prepare their heart, thou wilt cause thine ear to hear:

So Desire!

Every Woman in you Should _____!

Every Woman in you Should _____!

Every Woman in you Should _____!

Every Woman In You Should Breathe!

Ezekiel 37:5

Thus saith the Lord God unto these bones; Behold, I will cause breath to enter into you, and ye shall live:

So Breathe!

Every Woman in you Should _____!

Every Woman in you Should _____!

Every Woman In You Should Arise!

Mark 5:41

And he took the damsel by the hand, and said unto her, Talitha cumi; which is, being interpreted, Damsel, I say unto thee, arise.

So Arise!

Journals in the Keepsake Power Series:

Powerfully Peculiar
Be Made Whole
Wonderfully Made and Wonderfully God's

Journals in the Enduring Woman Series:

Every Woman In You Should____!
Endureth!
Unlayered and Free

For Individual Orders, visit us at: www.pecantreebooks.com.

For Bulk Orders, email us at: info@pecantreebooks.com

For literary and spiritual empowerment workshops,
contact E. Claudette Freeman, at: coaching@eclaudetteliterary.com or
visit the website, www.eclaudetteliterary.com.

www.ingramcontent.com/pod-product-compliance
Lightning Source LLC
LaVergne TN
LVHW051119080426
835510LV00018B/2121